D0760787

COLOSSEUM

Simon Rose

www.av2books.com

AV² provides enriched content that supplements and complements this book. Weigl's AV² books strive to create inspired learning and engage young minds in a total learning experience.

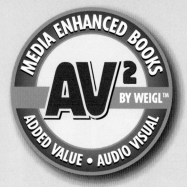

Go to **www.av2books.com,** and enter this book's unique code.

BOOK CODE

R658007

AV² by Weigl brings you media enhanced books that support active learning.

Your AV² Media Enhanced books come alive with...

Audio
Listen to sections of the book read aloud.

Video
Watch informative video clips.

Embedded Weblinks
Gain additional information for research.

Try This!
Complete activities and hands-on experiments.

Key Words
Study vocabulary, and complete a matching word activity.

Quizzes
Test your knowledge.

Slide Show
View images and captions, and prepare a presentation.

... and much, much more!

Published by AV² by Weigl
350 5th Avenue, 59th Floor
New York, NY 10118

Website: www.av2books.com   www.weigl.com

Library of Congress Cataloging-in-Publication Data

Rose, Simon, 1961-
  Colosseum / Simon Rose.
    p. cm. -- (Virtual field trip)
Includes index.
  ISBN 978-1-61913-249-8 (hardcover : alk. paper) -- ISBN 978-1-61913-255-9 (softcover : alk. paper)
  1. Colosseum (Rome, Italy)--Juvenile literature. 2. Amphitheaters--Rome--Juvenile literature.
  3. Rome (Italy)--Buildings, structures, etc.--Juvenile literature. I. Title.
  DG68.1.R67 2012
  937'.63--dc23

                        2011045453

Printed in the United States of America in North Mankato, Minnesota
1 2 3 4 5 6 7 8 9 0 16 15 14 13 12

012012
WEP060112

Editor: Heather Kissock
Design: Terry Paulhus

Every reasonable effort has been made to trace ownership and to obtain permission to reprint copyright material. The publishers would be pleased to have any errors or omissions brought to their attention so that they may be corrected in subsequent printings.

Weigl acknowledges Getty Images as its primary image supplier for this title.

Contents

What is the Colosseum?

The Colosseum stands tall in the heart of Rome, Italy. While now a ruin, it remains an impressive site. The structure represents both the glory and the cruelty that was once ancient Rome.

As an **amphitheater**, the Colosseum was built to stage events for the public. These events included **gladiator** fights and animal hunts. Up to 50,000 people would attend these events. They watched people compete in various contests, often to the death.

The real name of the building is the Flavian Amphitheater. It was named after the family of **emperors** that first built it in the late first century AD. The emperor Vespasian began work on the amphitheater in AD 72. It was completed eight years later.

The building was the scene of major events for centuries. As time went by, however, it was used less often. The Colosseum was eventually abandoned. Its stone was used in the construction of other buildings in Rome. Over the years, attempts have been made to restore the Colosseum to its original state. These efforts have met with varying levels of success.

The Flavian Amphitheater is better known as the Colosseum. It is believed that it received this name because of a large, or colossal, statue of the emperor Nero that once stood nearby.

Snapshot of Italy

Italy is a **peninsula** located in southern Europe. It includes a number of offshore islands, the largest of which are Sardinia and Sicily. Italy shares a northern border with France, Switzerland, Austria, and Slovenia. The rest of the country is surrounded by water. The Mediterranean and Ionian Seas are to the south, the Adriatic Sea to the east, and the Tyrrhenian Sea to the west.

INTRODUCING ITALY

CAPITAL CITY: Rome

FLAG:

POPULATION: 61,016,804 (2011)

OFFICIAL LANGUAGE: Italian

CURRENCY: Euro

CLIMATE: Mediterranean, with mild winters and warm summers. Winters can be cold at higher elevations.

SUMMER TEMPERATURE: 65° to 85° Fahrenheit (18° to 29° Celsius)

WINTER TEMPERATURE: 25° to 50° F (−4° to 10° C)

TIME ZONE: Central European Time (CET)

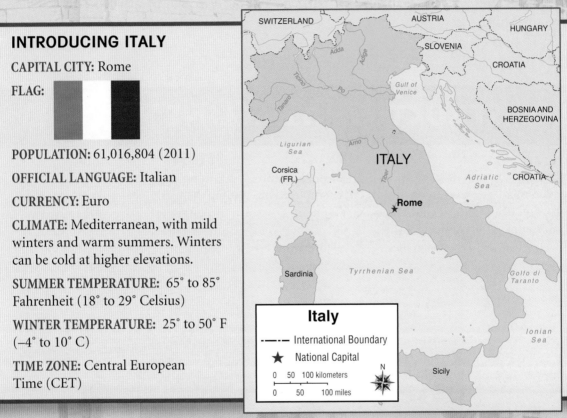

Italian Words to Know

When visiting a foreign country, it is always a good idea to know some words and phrases of the local language. Practice the phrases below to prepare for a trip to Italy.

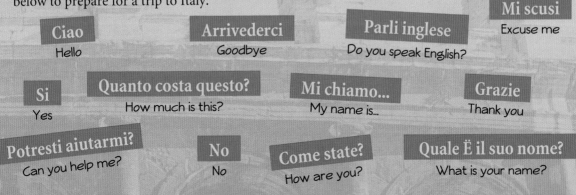

Ciao
Hello

Arrivederci
Goodbye

Parli inglese
Do you speak English?

Mi scusi
Excuse me

Si
Yes

Quanto costa questo?
How much is this?

Mi chiamo...
My name is...

Grazie
Thank you

Potresti aiutarmi?
Can you help me?

No
No

Come state?
How are you?

Quale È il suo nome?
What is your name?

A Step Back in Time

Vespasian became the Roman emperor after the reign of Nero. Nero had not been a respected ruler. He was known for his lack of concern for the citizens of Rome. The Colosseum was built on the site of Nero's former palace. Vespasian chose this location to show the people of Rome that he was a different type of ruler. He wanted to give back this part of the city to the people of Rome. In doing so, he believed that he would be popular with the people and that they would not rebel against him.

CONSTRUCTION TIMELINE

AD 72
Vespasian orders the construction of the Colosseum.

79
Three of the Colosseum's four stories have been completed when Vespasian dies.

80
The Colosseum is completed by Vespasian's son, Titus. To celebrate the opening of the Colosseum, Titus holds 100 days of games at the site.

82 to 96
Further changes are made to the building under Emperor Domitian.

217
The Colosseum is damaged by fire caused by lightning. It is repaired in the 240s and 250s.

Gladiator fights were part of the opening celebrations.

The Colosseum was also considered a monument to a recent victory. In AD 70, Vespasian and his son Titus stopped a revolt. They seized many treasures from the battle. Vespasian used his share of the riches to create the Colosseum. Roman rulers often had monuments built to celebrate great military victories.

The Colosseum was the largest amphitheater to be built in ancient Rome. It stood as a symbol of Vespasian's power as a ruler.

484 and 508
More work takes place on the building. It is believed to have been required following an earthquake.

1100s
The powerful local Frangipani family takes control of the Colosseum. They **fortify** it and then use it as a castle.

1800s
Repairs are made to the interior of the Colosseum.

1992 to 2000
Major restoration of the Colosseum takes place.

Restoration efforts continue in an effort to preserve the Colosseum remains. The building reopened in August 2010 after another round of maintenance.

The Colosseum Location

Rome is built on seven hills, and the Colosseum was constructed where the Palatine, Caelian, and Esquiline hills meet. At the time, the Colosseum was located very close to the Roman Forum. This was the political, religious, and commercial heart of the city.

To build the Colosseum, Vespasian had to clear the land and make it usable again. All remains of Nero's palace were taken down, and a large artificial lake that Nero had put in front of the palace was drained and filled in. The Colosseum was built where the lake once sat. Support buildings, such as stables and gladiator schools, were constructed on the rest of the grounds.

Placing an amphitheater in the middle of a city was rare. Most were built on the outskirts.

The Colosseum Today

The Colosseum continues to attract the masses almost 2,000 years after it was built. Millions of people visit the site every year, imagining how the structure must have appeared in ancient Rome. The building's original height can still be seen in the four-story section that is still standing. The sheer size of the structure is just one of the many testaments to this marvel of Roman **architecture**.

Height The Colosseum's outer wall is 160 feet (49 meters) high.

Area The base area of the Colosseum is more than 258,000 square feet (23,969 square meters). The **perimeter** of the outer wall was originally 1,788 feet (545 m).

Length and Width The Colosseum is oval in shape. It measures 620 feet (189 m) long and 513 feet (156 m) wide. The **arena** inside is 260 feet (79 m) long and 155 feet (47 m) wide.

513 feet (156 m)

160 feet (49 m)

Outside the Colosseum

Due to earthquakes and other damage, the Colosseum is only a portion of its original size. Still, the pieces that remain give visitors a glimpse into ancient Rome.

The triangular brick walls support what is left of the original perimeter wall at the north end of the structure.

Outer Wall The outer **façade** of the Colosseum is made of travertine, a form of limestone. Only the north section of the original outer wall remains. Triangular brick walls are found on the ends of the outer perimeter. They were added to the structure in the 19th century to protect the wall from further deterioration.

The arches on the second and third floors are believed to have once displayed statues of Roman gods and goddesses.

Arches The Colosseum's outer wall consists of three stories of **arcades**. The 80 arches at ground level served as entrances and exits to the building. Seventy-six of these archways were numbered to help people find their seats. The four remaining archways were reserved. The north main entrance was used only by the emperor and his guests. The other three archways were used by other high-ranking members of society and the gladiators.

Columns The arcades on the first three floors are separated by pillars that consist of a half column. Each floor has a different type of column. The first floor uses Doric columns. These slim, plain columns are capped with a simple disk. The second floor has Ionic columns. These columns feature a **scroll**-like decoration at the top. Corinthian columns adorn the third floor and the upper level of the structure. These columns are capped with elaborate sculptures.

The columns on the Colosseum's exterior are known as engaged columns. This means they have been built into the wall.

Promenades A series of promenades, or hallways, run around the inner wall of the Colosseum. People used these walkways to get to their seats. They could also gather in them to keep dry if it began to rain.

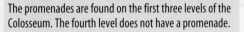

The promenades are found on the first three levels of the Colosseum. The fourth level does not have a promenade.

Upper Level The top level of the Colosseum is a solid wall with windows. Bronze shields used to rest between the windows as decoration. The Colosseum's upper level had 240 wooden beams. These supported a retractable **awning** called the velarium. The velarium could be pulled over the arena to protect the crowd from the Sun and the rain. It was operated by a team of 1,000 men.

The Upper Level was where women and commoners watched the games.

VIRTUAL TOUR

The Colosseum is open to the public throughout the year. The only days it is closed are Christmas Day and New Year's Day.

Inside the Colosseum

The interior of the Colosseum may be in ruins, but it is still an impressive sight. It is not difficult to imagine the stands filled with people watching an event unfold in the arena below.

Seating People from all walks of life came to watch events at the Colosseum. The seating plan, however, was arranged to reflect the different levels of Roman society. The most important people sat close to the arena. The lower classes sat higher up. Boxes were reserved for the emperor and his family and friends.

Important people sat on seats made from marble. Others sat on wooden seats or stood.

Today, a partial wooden floor covers the arena to show visitors how the Colosseum appeared when it was first built.

Arena The seating was arranged around the arena, which sat in the center of the Colosseum. The arena had a wooden floor that was covered with sand. Due to the dangerous nature of many of the events staged at the Colosseum, the arena was surrounded by metal grating. The grating was topped by elephant tusks and metal cylinders that rotated. The grating, tusks, and cylinders stopped wild animals from jumping from the arena into the crowd.

Tunnels also led into the arena.

Tunnels Tunnels from the hypogeum linked the Colosseum to places outside the building. These places included the gladiator training school, storage areas, and the stables where the animals were kept.

Hypogeum Underneath the arena's wooden floor was an area called the hypogeum. This was where the wild animals were kept before being brought into the arena to fight the gladiators. Gladiators and their weapons would also be housed below the arena until it was time to perform. It is believed that the people and the animals were brought up to the arena using **pulleys**. Those going to fight would be placed on a platform, and workers would lift the platform to the upper level using ropes.

The hypogeum contained a network of rooms, pens, hallways, and tunnels.

Audience members seated at the podium level were the closest to the action in the arena.

Podium The podium was the first **terrace** of seats around the arena. It was raised 11.7 feet (3.6 m) above the arena's floor, to both protect the spectators and to give them a better view. The podium was about 15 feet (4.6 m) wide. It was made up of a platform and seven rows of seating. The podium had the most spacious seating. Spectators in other sections were far more crowded.

Big Ideas Behind the Colosseum

Much planning went into the Colosseum before construction began. The builders needed to create a building that showcased the power of the Roman Empire and would stand the test of time.

Using his knowledge of ratios, the Colosseum's architect was able to place the columns evenly along the wall.

Ratios

When the architect began planning the Colosseum, he decided to base the size of the structure on the 5:3 ratio. A ratio measures the size of two things in relation to each other. In the case of the Colosseum, this ratio was used to plan a building that would be 300 by 180 **Roman feet**. Using this plan, the architect was able to determine the length of the building's perimeter and the number of arches on the outer wall. The basic design unit in ancient Rome was 20 Roman feet. Everything was designed using this measurement. The Colosseum's arches are 20 Roman feet wide. Due to the 5:3 ratio, the designer was able to determine that 80 arches could be placed in the outer walls.

Loads and Thrust

A building the size of the Colosseum must resist a great deal of pressure from the forces of load and thrust. A load is the total weight that a structure carries. It includes the materials used to create the building and any objects placed inside, such as people. The building had to be made to support all of the weight it would carry. Using a force called thrust, arches allowed the Colosseum to support all of its weight. Thrust is a force that pushes outward. The weight of the building bore down on the floors below, but the arches directed the force outward so that weight of the structure was spread evenly across a larger area.

The Colosseum's arches have helped the building survive through the centuries.

Science at Work in the Colosseum

Power tools did not exist in ancient Rome. Workers building the Colosseum had to rely on simple machines to help make their job easier.

Wheels and Axles

A special road was built from the **quarry** to the Colosseum construction site. The rock was taken there by oxen-pulled wagons. The wheels and axles on the wagons helped the oxen move the rock with ease. The wheel and axle is a two-part simple machine. It consists of a wheel with a rod, or axle, at its center. When the wheel is rotated, it turns the axle. This allows the structure upon which it sits to be moved easily. The wheel and axle help reduce the amount of **friction** between the ground and the object being moved. Only a small part of the wheel is ever on the ground. This means that the object does not rub against the ground as much. It moves more easily as a result.

About 200 oxen-pulled carts were used to transport rocks to the Colosseum.

The material a wedge is made from must be harder than the rock it is cutting. This ensures that the stone can be cut without breaking the wedge.

Wedges

The travertine that was used to build much of the Colosseum came from a quarry near the town of Tivoli. To cut the rock to size, the workers used a type of simple machine called a wedge. When edged in between two objects, a wedge pushes the two objects apart. Wedges make stonecutting easier by pushing apart two pieces of a rock. The rock splits at right angles away from the pointed part of the wedge.

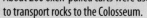

VIRTUAL TOUR

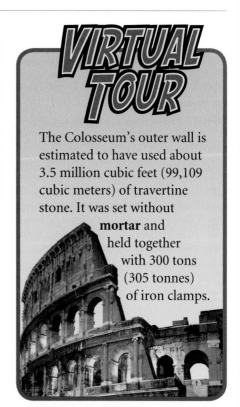

The Colosseum's outer wall is estimated to have used about 3.5 million cubic feet (99,109 cubic meters) of travertine stone. It was set without **mortar** and held together with 300 tons (305 tonnes) of iron clamps.

The Colosseum Builders

The architect of the Colosseum is unknown, but several Roman emperors were very involved in its initial construction and the changes that followed.

Titus Roman Emperor AD 79–81

Titus was Vespasian's oldest son. Due to his father's position, Titus was provided a formal

Titus worked closely with his father throughout his military career. He was seen as Vespasian's right-hand man.

education in the royal court. He then followed his father by embarking on a military career, working with Vespasian in the Middle East. When Vespasian became emperor, he named Titus his **successor**. Titus became emperor in AD 79 and continued the work of his father.

During his military career, Vespasian was stationed in various places, including Africa and Great Britain.

Vespasian Roman Emperor AD 69–79

Vespasian was the first emperor of the Flavian **dynasty**. He was not, however, born into a royal family. His father was a tax collector and banker. Vespasian embarked on a military career after he finished his schooling. While climbing the military ranks, he married and had two sons and one daughter. In AD 66, Nero sent Vespasian to quell a revolt in Jerusalem and Galilee. His success in this campaign eventually led him to become the emperor of Rome. As emperor, he worked to rebuild the city, launching several construction projects. He also expanded the Roman Empire in central Europe and the British Isles.

Domitian Roman Emperor AD 81–96

Titus was emperor for only two years. He died in AD 81 and was succeeded by his brother Domitian. As emperor, Domitian continued the work of his father and brother by rebuilding Rome. He was responsible for adding the uppermost level of the Colosseum. He also had the underground areas of the arena built.

Domitian was declared emperor the day after his brother died.

Building Contractors

Archaeologists have noted some small differences in how parts of the Colosseum seem to have been built. It is believed that each section was the work of four different teams of builders, all working at the same time. Today, companies often hire contractors to do jobs on a construction site. Building contractors are independent companies. They hire their own employees and purchase the materials they need to do their part of the job.

Contractors often specialize in specific construction tasks.

Laborers

A structure the size of the Colosseum required a large number of workers. It is believed that slaves were used as general laborers. They worked in the quarries and transported the travertine and marble to Rome. Laborers continue to play an important role on construction sites today. They know how to use tools, such as saws and hammers. They can also operate a variety of construction equipment.

Laborers can be found working in almost every area of construction.

Sculptors

Sculptors were responsible for crafting the statues that decorated the Colosseum. Sculptors create objects from materials such as marble and bronze. They usually draw a plan for the object they intend to create. Today, sculptors have the advantage of being able to use modern tools. In ancient Rome, sculptors' tools were very basic. They used chisels and simple hammers to create their works of art.

Some sculptors still use chisels and hammers in their work.

Similar Structures Around the World

The Colosseum has influenced the construction of buildings ever since it was built. Sports stadiums around the world have been constructed on the concept of an arena with the audience in stands around it. However, the Colosseum has also served as a model for other types of buildings.

Maracana Stadium

BUILT: 1948–1950
LOCATION: Rio de Janeiro, Brazil
DESIGN: Rafael Galvao, Pedro Paulo Bernardes Bastos, Orlando Azevedo, and Antonio Dias Carneiro
DESCRIPTION: The Maracana Stadium was built to host soccer's World Cup in 1950. It will host soccer again during the 2014 World Cup and will also be the main stadium for the 2016 Summer Olympics. The stadium held almost 200,000 spectators for the World Cup final in 1950, but currently has a capacity of about 80,000.

Maracana is the stadium's nickname. The stadium's official name is Estadio Jornalista Mario Filho. It was named after a well-respected Brazilian journalist.

Olympic Stadium

BUILT: 2007–2011
LOCATION: London, England
DESIGN: Populous Architects
DESCRIPTION: The London Olympic Stadium was the centerpiece of the Summer Olympic Games and Paralympics in 2012. It had a seating capacity of 80,000 for the events. The stadium is said to be the most **sustainable** ever built. It used less metal than previous stadiums, and much of it was recycled from other projects.

London's Olympic Stadium was the site of the opening and closing ceremonies for the 2012 Olympic Games.

Royal Albert Hall

BUILT: 1871
LOCATION: London, England
DESIGN: Francis Fowke and Henry Young Darracott Scott
DESCRIPTION: The Colosseum served as an inspiration for the builders of London's Royal Albert Hall. The hall hosts more than 350 musical performances every year, as well as numerous award ceremonies and charity events. The building can host events using its central arena or with a traditional stage at one end. It has held as many as 9,000 people, but now the capacity is limited to about 5,500.

Initially, Royal Albert Hall was supposed to seat 30,000 people. This number was reduced for both financial and practical reasons.

The Vancouver Public Library is part of Library Square. Several shops and eateries are also found in the complex.

Vancouver Public Library

BUILT: 1995
LOCATION: Vancouver, Canada
DESIGN: Moshe Safdie
DESCRIPTION: The exterior of the Vancouver Public Library holds a strong resemblance to the Colosseum in Rome as it stands today. The library itself is a square building, but it is surrounded by a free-standing oval-shaped wall. It is this wall that pays tribute to the Colosseum. The wall contains reading areas for library patrons. It is accessed by walkways that extend from the library's main building.

Issues Facing the Colosseum

At the time the Colosseum was built, there was little discussion about the environment. People did not worry about the effects the Colosseum's construction had on the surrounding area. They simply took what they needed and built where they wanted to build.

WHAT IS THE ISSUE?

The Colosseum is located in one of the world's largest cities, close to heavily used roads. It has suffered extensive damage from traffic pollution.

Acid rain is causing chemical damage to the Colosseum in the form of **corrosion**.

The Colosseum is one of the world's most popular tourist attractions and receives millions of visitors every year.

EFFECTS

Dark soot from vehicle exhaust fumes has blackened the outer walls of the Colosseum.

Black crusts have formed on parts of the Colosseum's walls. Acid in these crusts is eating away at the stone, weakening the structure.

The number of tourists that visit the Colosseum leads to a significant increase in humidity. This increase can result in **erosion** of the surrounding structure.

ACTION NEEDED

The latest round of restoration work on the Colosseum is scheduled to be completed by 2013. The outer walls will be cleaned, restoring the structure's natural color.

Acid rain will continue to be a problem for the Colosseum. The building must be cleaned regularly to prevent further damage.

In 2011, only 35 percent of the Colosseum was open to tourists due to safety concerns. Following the restoration program, more of the building will be open.

Make a Model of the Colosseum

The Colosseum is made from several types of rock. It took years to complete. You can make your own amphitheater in a day using the materials listed below.

Materials

- cardboard, cut in a
  12-inch (30.5-centimeter) square
- modeling clay
- drinking straws
- scissors
- terra cotta clay

Instructions

1. Place the cardboard on a flat surface.

2. Roll the modeling clay into a cord about 8 inches (20 cm) long and 1 inch (2.5 cm) thick. Arrange the clay in a circle in the middle of the cardboard.

3. Cut one of the drinking straws in half.

4. Bend one piece of the straw into an arch. The ends of the straw should be about 2 inches (5 cm) apart.

5. Press each end of the arched straw into the modeling clay so that the straw stands up.

6. Repeat this process until the straws fill the circle of clay.

7. Place a piece of modeling clay, about 1/2 inch (1.3 cm) tall, on the top of each arch.

8. Bend more pieces of straw, and press the ends into the clay on the arches.

9. Roll another ring of clay into a cord and place over the second ring of arches.

10. Cover the entire surface of the structure with terra cotta clay and let dry.

11. Display your Colosseum for all to see.

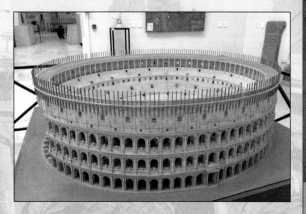

Colosseum Quiz

Q Who ordered the construction of the Colosseum?

A Emperor Vespasian.

Q What types of events were held at the Colosseum?

A Gladiator fights and animal hunts

Q How many entrances did the Colosseum have?

A 80. Four were reserved for important people. The remaining 76 were for the general public.

Q What is a velarium?

A A velarium is a type of awning. It was pulled over the Colosseum's seating area to protect people from the Sun and rain.

Words to Know

acid rain: the result of a chemical transformation which occurs after sulphur dioxide and nitrogen oxides are emitted into the air and absorbed by water droplets in the clouds

amphitheater: an oval or circular building with rising rows of seats arranged about an open space

arcades: a series of arches supported by columns

architecture: the art and science of designing and erecting buildings

arena: a circular or oval shaped area for staging performances or other events, surrounded by seating on all sides

awning: a rooflike shelter made of canvas

corrosion: the process of eating or wearing away

dynasty: a family or group that maintains power for several generations

emperors: rulers of the Roman Empire

erosion: the wearing away of rocks, soil, etc. by the action of water, ice, or wind

façade: the face of a building

fortify: to make strong

friction: the rubbing of one surface against another

gladiator: someone who fought in the amphitheaters of the Roman Empire for public entertainment

mortar: a building material like cement that hardens to hold objects together

peninsula: a piece of land that juts into a body of water

perimeter: continuous line forming a boundary around the outside of an object or space

pulleys: simple machines consisting of grooved wheels and ropes that are used to move objects up or down

quarry: an open pit from which stone is obtained

Roman feet: a length of about 11.6 inches (29.5 centimeters)

scroll: a roll of paper

successor: a person who follows another in a position or office

sustainable: capable of being continued with minimal effect on the environment

terrace: a porch or walkway bordered by columns

Index

Log on to www.av2books.com

AV² by Weigl brings you media enhanced books that support active learning. Go to www.av2books.com, and enter the special code found on page 2 of this book. You will gain access to enriched and enhanced content that supplements and complements this book. Content includes video, audio, weblinks, quizzes, a slide show, and activities.

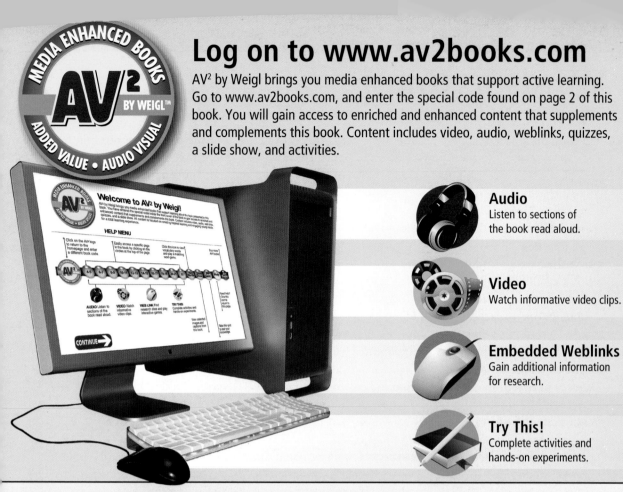

Audio
Listen to sections of the book read aloud.

Video
Watch informative video clips.

Embedded Weblinks
Gain additional information for research.

Try This!
Complete activities and hands-on experiments.

WHAT'S ONLINE?

Try This!	Embedded Weblinks	Video	EXTRA FEATURES
Identify the features of the Colosseum.	Learn more about the Colosseum and the activities it hosted.	Watch a video to discover the engineering secrets behind the Colosseum.	**Audio** Listen to sections of the book read aloud.
Imagine that you are designing the Colosseum.	Find out how the Colosseum has changed over time.	Watch a video to learn more about Roman architecture.	**Key Words** Study vocabulary, and complete a matching word activity.
Test your knowledge of the Colosseum.	See what the Colosseum looked like when it was first built.		**Slide Show** View images and captions, and prepare a presentation.
			Quizzes Test your knowledge.

AV² was built to bridge the gap between print and digital. We encourage you to tell us what you like and what you want to see in the future.

Sign up to be an AV² Ambassador at www.av2books.com/ambassador.